CHANGE
a constant challenge

John Maclean

with Juliet Rogers

T0359487

CHANGE
a constant
challenge

John Maclean
with Juliet Rogers

A John Maclean book for Simon & Schuster Australia

Many of us have internal conversations, discussions with ourselves, constantly throughout each day. These conversations can sometimes be counterproductive and limit our ability to move forward. I hope the insights I've gathered in this book will help readers commit to changing the conversation and embracing a more supportive internal dialogue.

John Maclean

Contents

In a split second

In 1988, while training for the Nepean Triathlon, I was hit by a truck – not metaphorically, but literally – and in a split second my life changed completely. I went from being a professional footballer, someone who was born to run, to a paraplegic facing a future without the use of my legs. Pretty confronting for a 22-year-old. After the initial shock and despair had started to abate, I came to understand that because of where the breaks in my spine had occurred, and how my spinal cord had been damaged, I was what is termed an incomplete paraplegic, meaning that I still retained some movement and feeling in my legs. This was the lifeline that I desperately needed, and I grabbed it with both hands: I made a pledge that at the end of my treatment I was going to walk out of hospital.

After months of painful and frustrating rehab, I did fulfil that dream, with more than a little help from my forearm crutches. Fuelled by the desire to resume my old life, I did everything that I possibly could to regain the use of my legs. I trained harder than I'd ever trained before, but the day came when I finally had to face the fact that all the determination in the world wasn't going to give me back the full use of my legs.

Over the next few years, I focused on transforming myself into a wheelchair athlete.

Embrace the new

As the world around me implodes in the face of the global coronavirus pandemic, I've suddenly found myself with a lot of time on my hands for reflection on the impact that this huge event is having on my life – and on the lives of the people around me. I've experienced a lot of change since the accident that led to my paraplegia over 30 years ago, and through these experiences I've learned how to *embrace* the new, not *fear* it.

I wasn't completely aware of it at the time, but with the benefit of hindsight I can now look back to where it all began and see that I've developed a methodology for managing change that has helped me conquer the challenges I've been drawn to throughout my life. I believe that in this time of fear and disruption, when so many of you are facing an uncertain and turbulent future, my methodology could help.

So, I'm going to start by taking you back to 1994, when I set out on my big challenge to become the first wheelchair athlete to complete the Ironman Triathlon World Championship in Kona, Hawaii. The lessons I learned then are the foundation stones that I've used to manage change ever since.

Welcome to change, the John Maclean way

Where it all began

Swim 2.4 miles! Bike 112 miles! Run 26.2 miles! Brag for the rest of your life!

John Collins, founder, Hawaiian Ironman

Don't fear the new.
Embrace it.

I've got fond memories of sitting on the lounge room floor at home as a young boy, glued to the television, watching the coverage of the Ironman World Championship. I was fascinated by the strength and endurance of the competitors and inspired by the way they could push their bodies to such limits, and I dreamed that one day I would be one of those athletes.

When I had my accident, that dream seemed over. Competing in a triathlon without the use of my legs was impossible. Or so I thought.

In 1994, I was once again watching the Ironman race, when two things happened: Greg Welch, a fellow Australian, won the race; and Jon Franks, an American, lined up as the first wheelchair athlete to attempt the course. Although Franks failed to meet the qualifying time for the bicycle leg and decided not to complete the event, he'd still given it a go. The impossible seemed possible once again. Suddenly, there it was, my next challenge: I was going to be the first wheelchair athlete to complete the Hawaiian Ironman.

Given that it's one of the toughest endurance races in the world, most people would consider this the height of masochism. But for me this event met a need for acceptance – it offered me a chance to be seen as equal again.

At the time, I believed I'd come a long way, and in many respects I had. I'd gradually accepted that the wheelchair actually gave me more freedom to develop new skills than struggling along on crutches was ever going to provide. I had a job I enjoyed. I was training hard and making real progress in kayaking, the new sport that I'd taken on. I was setting myself other new challenges – including participation in the Nepean Triathlon, the race I'd been training for when I had my accident, and the Sri Chinmoy Triathlon, which was almost double the length of the Nepean event – and I was getting a real sense of satisfaction every time I knocked one of them over.

I was going to be the first wheelchair athlete to complete the Hawaiian Ironman

I was certainly focused and determined, but following every challenge I found that my sense of accomplishment didn't last long. I had a constant need to prove to myself, and everyone else, that I was equal – the beast kept needing to be fed. I was convinced that the Hawaiian Ironman event was the answer, and I was going to put everything I could into crossing that finish line. Not just for my self-esteem, but also to inspire kids in wheelchairs all around the world to believe that their chair didn't have to curtail their dreams.

At first glance, the map for success seemed clear. Swim 3.8 kilometres. Bike 180 kilometres. Run 42.2 kilometres. Complete it all under 17 hours, and hear my name called as I crossed the finish line: *John Maclean, you are an IRONMAN!*

If only it were that simple.

I'd learned important lessons from my earlier challenges. Initially, I hadn't really appreciated the key role that nutrition plays in endurance racing, and I found out the hard way that undertaking such an event without supplies of food and drink will lead to dehydration and loss of energy. Preparation is everything.

The other lesson I'd learned was more personal. The Nepean Triathlon was my first significant public race, and the closer that event got, the more concerned I became. As the only guy in a wheelchair, I was embarrassed about my 'difference', and didn't want everyone to see me being carried to the start line of the swim leg. I mentioned to a friend that I was thinking about completing the course the day before the event, to prove to myself that I could do it, but without having to endure the curiosity of the crowd. Unsurprisingly, my mate – who'd trained with me every inch of the way – was unimpressed by that suggestion

The problem had only ever been in my head ... to hell with what other people think!

and pointed out, in no uncertain terms, that he hadn't struggled out of bed each morning to train with me only to have me bail at the last minute. So, I swallowed my pride and competed along with everyone else – and realised how ridiculous I'd been. The problem had only ever been in my head. That was my second important lesson: to hell with what other people think!

Making the decision to take on the Hawaiian Ironman had been straightforward, but I was soon to discover that the broader plan would be a little more complicated. I'd no idea how to even go about entering the event.

I knew that Jon Franks had completed the Surfers Paradise International Triathlon the previous year, and after some thought I decided that my first step would be to have a crack at the same race. I'd then be able to compare our times and assess if I was in with a chance to qualify for the big race.

When I bettered Franks' time by 45 minutes, I got all the encouragement I needed to take the next step.

The next stage of the plan was to find out what I needed to do to enter the competition. I wrote to the race director to find out how to go about qualifying for the Ironman, and discovered that I would have to race off against Franks in the Gulf Coast Triathlon (half the distance of the Hawaiian Ironman) in Panama City, Florida, in order to get the green light. So, with many months of training under my belt, I headed for Florida, my gateway to the Ironman.

Race day arrived and I was feeling confident. I finished the swim in first place across the physically challenged (PC) field, which had started before everybody else – an achievement that was somewhat undermined by my race supporter nosediving into the sand as he piggybacked me to the start of the cycle leg! After recovering both my dignity and my sense of humour, I set off strongly on my handcycle, still in the lead, but by the time I'd clocked up 5 kilometres, the elite athletes started to zip past me with ease. Despite this, my mission was accomplished – not only because Jon Franks pulled out at the end of the cycle race, but also because I completed the course in 5 hours, 40 minutes. I was off to compete in the 1995 Ironman. All I had to do now was double my Gulf Coast Triathlon time to 11 hours, 20 minutes for the full Hawaiian Ironman event. A breeze!

I returned to Panama City, a month before the Kona event, to train in the same heat and humidity that I would encounter in Hawaii. I'd received an invitation to stay with a friend, who worked on the organising committee for the Gulf Coast Triathlon. This seemed a great opportunity, until reality hit.

Dave picked me up at the airport in his pickup truck, and while we were chatting he mentioned that it was going to be a tight squeeze at his house. I guess he hadn't expected the pile of luggage that goes along with being a wheelchair triathlete: a day chair to get around in, a handcycle and a racing wheelchair, together with extra racing wheels, a swim bag with wetsuit, and a few more bags full of clothes. When we arrived at the house, I saw that there was no garage – so nowhere to put all my paraphernalia – and that a small set of stairs led up to the front door, which meant I couldn't get into the house without help. I was in trouble.

That evening, another friend, Denise Centrone, came to pick me up to attend a party. I mentioned my plight – feeling a little sick in my stomach, as I had no Plan B. She immediately suggested that we go and talk to her mum, Lynn. Lynn lived alone, having lost her husband in a plane accident. When I recounted my predicament, Lynn invited me to stay with her in her five-bedroom house, all on one level, complete with a double garage to store all my stuff. This was the perfect spot for me to train. I had a local pool nearby, and countless places to ride my handcycle and push my racing wheelchair. Greatly relieved, I moved in, and Lynn and I became good friends, often taking late afternoon walks/wheels and solving the problems of the world. I have such fond memories of our time together, and I'll always be so grateful for her generosity.

Indeed, I'd been fortunate to have wonderful people throughout my life, both family and friends, who'd supported me unconditionally. But, before my accident, I was fiercely independent, and asking for help was a concept foreign to me. It was therefore a huge challenge for me to adjust to the changes that becoming a paraplegic presented, in terms of everyday tasks that I'd always taken for granted. I had to learn how to dress myself, manoeuvre a wheelchair, navigate small rises and drive a car in a new way, but I also had to learn how to ask for help. Navigating a flight of stairs in a wheelchair could not be done on my own, regardless of my desire for independence.

It took me a long time to understand that needing help is not a sign of weakness – and that asking for it in a direct and open way is an invaluable skill for anyone to have, as there are times when we all need a helping hand. Indeed, this journey of discovery really began during my time at Panama City, where I learned that when you open yourself up to others, you'll be surprised by the generosity and support you receive.

It took me a long time to understand that needing help is not a sign of weakness

Starting with the kindness of both Dave and Lynn, during my Ironman preparation I met so many people who went on to play a major part in my life, both practically and emotionally, as mentors, supporters and lifelong friends. I didn't plan for any of this to happen, but I count myself incredibly lucky that it did. These key people included an emergency doctor I'd met at a dinner, who offered to help me financially and made good on that offer by paying for a new racing chair, which I couldn't have afforded otherwise. I also talked to as many people as I could find who'd previously completed the race, in order to discover as much as possible about the challenge I was facing. Their willingness to share that knowledge was heart-warming.

Only ten months after the idea had first popped into my head, I flew off to Kona, Hawaii for the race of my life: a 13- to 17-hour adventure unfolding over 226 kilometres. The day of the event dawned at last and – with a supportive team of family and friends around me – the preparation began, somewhat differently for me than for the other athletes. They probably didn't have to go through the less than pleasant task of inserting a catheter, nor did they have to worry about donning a wetsuit, the one concession accorded me to help with buoyancy, given I was unable to kick my legs like everyone else.

I'd allowed myself plenty of time to check all my equipment prior to the 7 am start, and finally it was time for my two mates to carry me down to the water for the beginning of the first leg. As helicopters buzzed overhead and the air reverberated with the excitement of 1,500 athletes and their many supporters, I readied myself for the starting cannon to go off. Before the smoke had even cleared, the ocean turned into a giant washing machine as all the competitors headed off, swimming over anyone who got in their way. I was so hyped that by the time I reached the first marker **I gradually calmed myself down and continued at a steady pace that I could maintain** I was gasping for air. I gradually calmed myself down and continued at a steady pace that I could maintain throughout the leg, especially now that the field had spread out and I was at less risk of a collision.

I remember telling myself to reach and pull through each stroke, just as I'd done during training: *reach and pull, reach and pull*. I looked up a few times on the way to the turnaround point – but every time, that marker seemed so far away. With the *reach and pull* mantra playing in my head, however, I managed to keep up a good rhythm, and was finally rewarded when I saw two boats anchored together: the halfway point, at last. All the swimmers were massing together, battling for the best position and the straightest line, but somehow I managed to negotiate the turnaround point without being mowed over. It was now time to conserve energy as I headed for home, or, at least, the end of the swim leg.

As I swam on, my mind drifted back to the day when I was wheeled into the rehab unit's hydrotherapy pool for the first time. I'd transferred from my day wheelchair to a plastic wheelchair before being lowered down the ramp into the water. The physio supported me with floats to prevent me from sinking. It took everything I had to swim a few strokes, before being wheeled back up the ramp. I was completely exhausted, and it was such a relief to be back in bed and able to rest. Yet here I was now, swimming towards the finish of the first leg of the Ironman. That did great things for my motivation, I can tell you.

I completed the swim in 1 hour, 7 minutes, not far behind the 50 minutes achieved by the elite athletes, which filled me with confidence that I would finish the course by midnight.

Looking back on this race, with the benefit of nearly 25 years more experience, I'm in two minds as to whether to applaud my determination and chutzpah, or cringe in embarrassment at my naivety in allowing one of my supporters to apply Vaseline under my arms before wiping the rest on the back of my neck – a really clever idea, given the intensity of the Hawaiian sun.

I started the cycling in a good frame of mind, buoyed by the crowds, happily oblivious to the reality that using your arms – rather than your thighs – to propel yourself up a hill is a lot more challenging than I'd taken into consideration. I then hit the Queen K (the Queen Ka'ahumanu Highway), and everything began to change. I was surrounded by black volcanic rubble, and the heat was intense – particularly on a handcycle that sits so close to the ground. But it was the wind that began to do me in. Gusts of up to 100 kilometres an hour swirled across the road, and my spirits were nosediving.

I remember trying to focus on maintaining a steady pace, when a local Hawaiian, riding an upright cruiser bike complete with streamers on the handlebar grips, came up beside me. He looked like he was heading off to buy an ice-cream, rather than competing in a triathlon. He greeted me, commented on the beautiful weather, and then continued up the next rise on the course. I tried as hard as I could to catch up to him on the short downhill section, feeling very pleased with myself when I did just that – but my satisfaction was short-lived. On another uphill section, there he was again, smiling happily as he rode past me. This time I couldn't keep up with him, as the incline just kept on going, but it seemed to me he had the perfect attitude. He was making the most of the opportunity to compete as a local, and while I was fighting my own frustration, as well as the elements, he was taking it all in and enjoying his day. I didn't see him again after he rode away from me that second time, but the moment stayed with me as a perfect illustration of the importance of a positive mindset.

To make matters worse, not only did I have to contend with being overtaken again, and again, and again, by cyclists coming up from behind me, but I also had to endure the sight of the frontrunners whizzing by me on the other side of the road after having reached the halfway point. With the wind behind them, their speed was both impressive and deeply depressing.

Some five hours after setting out, I was tired, sore and increasingly concerned about my ability to meet the cut-off time for this leg – and I'd only just reached the halfway point. To add insult to injury, the wind had now turned yet again, and I was cycling right into the teeth of it. I was in a world of pain, physically and mentally, but somehow I kept those wheels turning. Try as I might, it didn't take long until my arms started cramping as I pushed myself way beyond any comfort zone I'd known before. If I paused, even briefly, my biceps or triceps (depending on whether I was pushing or pulling on the hand cranks) would go into spasm, so of course I then tried not to pause at all.

It seemed to me he had the perfect attitude ... taking it all in and enjoying his day

I was well and truly over the initial excitement of racing Ironman and would have given anything to be back in my hotel room watching it on TV. As I faced the headwinds again, there was so much running through my mind. I thought back to the time when I'd finally moved from ICU into the spinal unit, sharing a ward with three other guys who'd broken their necks and could do nothing at all on their own. They would have given anything to change places with me and have the freedom to use their arms. I was lucky to be alive. I was lucky not to have suffered brain damage. I was lucky that I still had full use of my upper body. This certainly gave me back my sense of perspective, stopping my pity party dead in its tracks. By changing that narrative in my head, I was able to completely change my mindset and remind myself why I'd taken on the challenge in the first place: to be seen as equal and to inspire kids in wheelchairs.

I kept moving forward until, as twilight fell and Kona once again came into view, I had to face the fact that I couldn't meet the cut-off time.

I can still feel the despair that washed over me at that point. All that work – and all for nothing. I was completely undone.

Then one of my mates from the support team was asked to come and tell me that although I'd missed the qualifying time, the organisers were going to allow me to finish the race. It was pretty hard to appreciate the generosity of that gesture right then, I can tell you, when every inch of my body was screaming at me to make it all stop. I just wanted to go home. And then my mate said: *It's my son's birthday today, but I came here to support you. You've got to go on. You're going to have to give it a bit more.* In the face of that level of support, after ten hours on my handcycle,

Somehow ... the encouragement of the right words, at the right time, had me heading for that finish line

what choice did I have but to grind on to the transition station and ready myself for the 42.2-kilometre marathon that still awaited me.

This was my first-ever marathon, and it didn't take long for it to feel as though it would also be my last, especially when I hit my first hill. However hard I tried, I couldn't get any traction, and I could see no way that I could make it up that rise. Following a suggestion from my mates, I turned the chair around and, inch by inch, worked my way up the incline backwards. I made it to the top, but – you guessed it – after the brief respite of a downwards run, there was another hill. Halfway up, I stopped, convinced that this really was it and that going on was impossible. *I'm not enjoying this anymore*, I said to my mate – one of the biggest understatements I've ever made. To which I got the response: *The pain won't last forever, but the memories will.*

Somehow, even though I was running on empty, the encouragement of the right words, at the right time, had me heading for that finish line. I even started to catch up with some of the other athletes as my racing chair picked up momentum, especially going downhill, which was a huge recharge for my confidence. All the competitors, even the athletes who'd completed the race some hours ago, had come back to show their support for those of us who were yet to finish, and the volunteers were still providing hydration, nutrition and energy as we went past their aid stations. As I turned onto that final stretch of road, I took out my little Australian flag, which I'd taped to my racing chair. I felt a sense of enormous pride as I waved it as hard as I could while being cheered to the finish line, where I at last heard those wonderful words: *John Maclean, you are an IRONMAN!*

So, despite missing the cut-off time, I reached the finish line 14 hours, 52 minutes after I set out and 2 hours, 8 minutes before the midnight deadline. Not quite the 11-hour jaunt I'd envisaged when I qualified, but every bit as sweet.

That achievement meant so much to me. I felt more confident and had a greater sense of equality. But, as my body repaired itself over the coming months, the *what if*s in my head became louder. *What if* I'd been more prepared, trained harder, had better equipment? *What if* the conditions hadn't resulted in cyclonic winds that blew competitors from their bikes? Utterly futile, of course, but the only way to answer those questions became my new challenge: it was time to give the event another crack.

This time the qualification race was held in Santa Rosa, in California, and as the only wheelchair entrant all I had to do was finish the race, which I duly did. I was off to Kona again.

When I'd started the race the previous year, I'd been full of confidence – but as I lined up for the start in 1996, I couldn't rid myself of the sense that something wasn't right. The swim went well, as did the cycle leg – until, with 50 kilometres left to ride, I blew a tyre. Not a biggie, except that I was in the middle of the Queen K in blistering heat and couldn't sit on the tarmac to change the tyre without risking burning myself badly (and probably without even realising it, given the lack of sensitivity in parts of my legs). I had no choice but to limp towards the next aid station, 5 kilometres away. The 20 minutes that this incident ended up taking saw me miss the cut-off time for that leg of the event.

I was once again allowed to complete the race, cutting 13 minutes off my 1995 time, and as I crossed the finish line, someone slipped a finisher's medal around my neck. Of course, when the cold light of day hit me the next morning, I realised that the medal had been a mistake. I hadn't completed the race in the required times and I had to return the medal. What counts the most is what you do when no one is watching.

Returning to Australia, I tried to convince myself that I'd done enough to prove I could complete that gruelling event – twice! – and that I needed to move on. But I just couldn't do it. In the words immortalised by Sir Edmund Hillary, *I had to knock the bastard off*.

I prepared for my third Ironman challenge with a new level of intensity. Support from my many friends and sponsors had helped me to develop a new career as a public speaker, allowing me to become a full-time athlete. I was therefore able to train even more ferociously, and I had much better equipment. But as I headed towards my third attempt, there were some changes that made this 1997 Ironman even more significant. Six athletes were contesting the three available spots in the qualifying race in Texas, and for the first time the wheelchair category for Hawaii was made official. I managed to qualify second, so I'd now be racing two other athletes as well as those cut-off times.

This time round, I completed the swim leg in an hour – my best time yet – and I met the cut-off time for the cycle leg, ahead of my other two competitors. Just the marathon leg to go. Despite depleting my strength with six bouts of vomiting after a bad reaction to an energy drink, I reached that finish line, as the winner of my category, in 12 hours, 21 minutes. That was the sweetest victory of them all.

Yesterday I was clever, so I wanted to change the world. Today I am wise, so I am changing myself.

Rumi

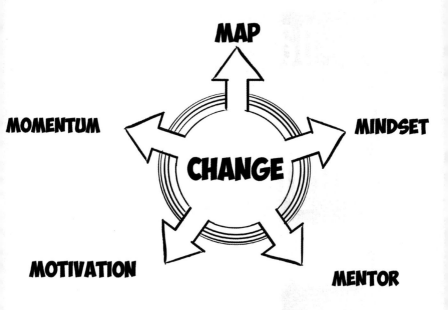

The path to managing change

Wanna fly, you got to give up
the shit that weighs you down.

Toni Morrison, *Song of Solomon*

See it.
Believe it.
Achieve it.

So, it all started with the Hawaiian Ironman. Driven by a need for acceptance (my own, as much as everyone else's), by naivety, determination, ego and a desire to give back, I learned lessons that set me on a path to managing change. Out of this experience I began to develop the building blocks that have helped me embrace change – as well as an understanding that the big wins only come in life when you step out of your comfort zone and give everything you have to chasing your dreams.

I learned the importance of planning well and being prepared. I learned that I could control the inner voice that so often undermines us: the internal narrative telling us that we're not good enough and that we can't achieve what we're trying to do. I learned the importance of surrounding myself with positive people who lifted me up, who would be there through thick and thin, with the right words, at the right moment, to keep me on my path. I learned that determination and resilience can overcome pain and despair. I learned to draw on the experience of others to expand my knowledge and increase my chances of success. And I learned that once you build momentum, you can move mountains.

So, what's my recipe for embracing change?

Map	Developing the plan that will guide you to your destination.
Mindset	Turning that negative voice in your head into a positive one, and becoming open to new experiences and new opportunities.
Mentor	Getting help from experienced people who have succeeded before you, and understanding that this is a sign of strength: you don't have to go it alone.
Motivation	Finding and maintaining the sense of purpose that drives you to aim for your dream and step onto the hard road.
Momentum	Staying the course, building on each success and measuring your progress.

By following these guiding principles, I've been able to grow and achieve in an ever-changing world – and if I can do it, I believe that you can too.

MAP

A goal without a plan is just a wish.

Antoine de Saint Exupéry

Knowing where you want to go is an important start, but even the best intention is not enough on its own. Your goal can only become a reality when you create a detailed and realistic plan for change.

I was thrilled when I finally conquered the Hawaiian Ironman course within the stipulated times, becoming the first wheelchair athlete to do so, but it wasn't long before the 'Ironman blues' set in. That race had consumed me for almost three years – and then there was a void. Not one to rest on my laurels, I decided that it was time to gather my resources and set myself a new challenge:

to swim the English Channel. This had long been a dream of mine, but when I learned that not only had no wheelchair athlete ever achieved it, but neither had any Hawaiian Ironman, the opportunity to set both those records was irresistible.

With my Channel swim, there were many factors to take into account in the planning. I had to work out the best time of year to undertake the challenge, as weather was obviously going to be a critical factor. I was going to have to swim a very long way, so the right training in the right conditions was equally as important: there was no point in being able to swim a huge number of lengths of a perfectly calm pool. I also needed to beef up, by at least 20 kilograms, to increase my resistance to the cold. A big 'map' calls for a large support team, and to help plot a route that gave me the best chance of success my team included a coach, nutritionist, physiotherapist and support swimmers. And then there were the myriad practical details that had to be sorted out.

After seven months of hard training and extensive planning, the day finally arrived. At 5 am, full of equal parts trepidation and excitement, I entered the water at Dover and set off for France. I had the very best support and the very best plan, but by the time I was six hours into the crossing, the wind had picked up to such an extent that it was at Force 8 level. Given that Force 12 is deemed to be a hurricane, it's no surprise that, however hard I tried, I was making no progress. After I'd been in the water for nine hours, I had to face the news that for the past three hours I'd in fact been dropping back.

Pitted against the relentless force of nature, there was no alternative but to admit defeat, and after ten hours I abandoned my attempt and was pulled from the water into the support boat. I was so exhausted that I slept most of the next week. But I couldn't let the challenge go – it was time to try again. Some two weeks later, I set off on my second attempt, finally reaching France in 12 hours, 55 minutes.

Swimming the English Channel is as good an example of the need for a map, both literally and figuratively, as you can get, and while it's unlikely that your goal is to conquer the Channel – although if it is, just give me a call – the principles of a good plan are universal.

Do your research

Seek out examples of people who've already succeeded in achieving your chosen goal, or a similar one. Read as widely as you can and talk to as many people as possible, until you're confident that you understand what needs to be done and, even more importantly, the best way of going about it.

When I was researching for the Channel swim, I found out that wetsuits weren't permitted in any official Channel crossing. Of course, I wanted my attempt to be official, but the absence of a wetsuit was going to make swimming without the use of my legs considerably more difficult. I'm grateful to this day that the organisers ultimately agreed to a dispensation, to give me back a little of the buoyancy that most swimmers achieve with their legs. But had I not done my homework, I may well not have discovered that unwelcome news until I was about to set off on the challenge.

Be realistic about your skills and abilities

You can't make a good plan if you're not honest about what you're good at and what you're not. I don't mean that you shouldn't stretch yourself, but if you struggle to get from one end of the pool to the other without pausing for breath, then a Channel swim is probably not the right goal for you. Be as ruthlessly honest as you can, because the aim is to succeed, and lying to yourself about your abilities isn't going to help you do that.

Be precise

As you begin to scope out your plan in detail, you must think about the steps that you need to take and map out the right route. Be realistic, timely and specific, otherwise you won't be able to measure your success. Ask yourself the following questions:

- *When should I start?*

- *Where should I start?*

- *What resources do I need?*

- *How long is it going to take?*

Prepare for the unexpected and have a Plan B

What happens if something goes wrong? What's your Plan B, and under what circumstances should it come into play? This doesn't mean that you're planning to fail, but even the best-laid plans can go awry, often through no fault of your own. So, it's important that you recognise when that curve ball is coming your way, and that you've given some thought to how you might prevent it derailing everything.

It's probably easiest to think of your plan in terms of a literal map. I'm sure that, like me, you've all had the experience of driving along with your sat nav on, and then turning right as instructed, only to find that you've hit a dead end – or that all the traffic is heading towards you as you turn into a one-way street, going in the wrong direction.

After telling your navigation system exactly what you think, you get off that road as quickly as possible, stop and regroup, and plan a different course to the same destination.

It's the same with your plan. If you're not meeting the milestones that you've set, you need to have the courage to stop, draw breath, and work out what's gone wrong and how you're going to put it right. Plan B is a very helpful thing.

Tomorrow belongs to the people who prepare for it today.

African proverb

MINDSET

Open the window of your mind. Allow the fresh air, new lights and new truths to enter.

Amit Ray, *Walking the Path of Compassion*

Mindset is the voice inside your head that informs your attitude to life. If you have a strong, positive mindset and view the world with optimism, it's a great tool for change. But if that small voice keeps delivering a string of negatives, the idea of change will seem scary, and you'll find it harder and harder to try something new.

Always remember that you have choice. You may not be able to change what has happened in the past, but you can most definitely control the way you respond in the future. Of course you have to be aware of that inner dialogue first, but once you've identified it, you can make the decision to turn that negative voice into one of encouragement and hope. It won't happen at the flick of a switch, but if you persevere, your inner voice can become your biggest ally in change.

We all have a mindset that has built up over time through our experiences:

I suck at sport.

I can't do maths.

I'm a lousy public speaker.

If you have a fixed mindset, you hold on to the belief that your personality is what it is and can't be changed. It's no surprise that failure to succeed in doing something different is then almost guaranteed. But if you develop a growth mindset – by changing that narrative in your head, that internal voice that tells you not to bother trying because you've failed in the past – then you can make some of those roadblocks disappear.

So, when that voice kicks in, start to question it:

What's the worst thing that can happen if I take this new step and it doesn't work out?

How will I feel if I don't try?

The really telling question for me has always been: *How would I feel if I didn't give something a go?* Ask yourself this, and you'll be amazed how often the fear of failure looms much larger than the scariness of the new step that you're considering.

As I learned when I confronted the challenges of the Hawaiian Ironman competition, by changing the conversation inside my head I was able to shift my mindset and carry on with the race with renewed commitment. By doing this, I avoided having to face the crushing sense of failure I would have experienced if I'd pulled out of the event.

Remember, you don't have to do this on your own. If you surround yourself with the right people, they can lift you up at just the right moment. By the right people, I mean the people you respect and whose opinions you value. They mightn't be the people you expect, but they need to have the courage to speak up, even when they know you want them to support a different decision. My mate did it for me in the Kona race – *The pain won't last, but the memories will* – and he was absolutely right.

But it's not just friends and family who can influence your mindset. It's also those experienced people who've already travelled the path that you want to take. When I was starting out as a rower, I was fortunate enough to meet Drew Ginn, an Olympic rower and triple gold medallist, and his words of advice have stayed with me ever since. He told me that when he has a big race coming up, he switches on *when he gets in the boat*, whereas most people will overprocess and overanalyse *in the lead-up* to a big competition. By the time they hit the start line, they're already tired. As a newcomer to the sport, that was exactly what I was doing. Once I became aware of the problem, I worked hard to switch my mind off in the lead-up to an event and save my energy for the race.

The really telling question for me has always been: How would I feel if I didn't give something a go?

I've experienced a lot of change over the years – football player, wheelchair triathlete, kayaker, marathon swimmer, wheelchair racer, fundraiser, sailor, handcyclist, endurance paddler, rower and now the world's slowest triathlete – and each time I've embarked on a new challenge, I've had to develop a new mindset.

When I had my accident, I initially had huge trouble getting my head around the fact that I was never going to walk again. Until that moment, my legs had been my passport to success, as it was my speed that enabled me to develop a career as a professional athlete. I was utterly focused on that career: I knew where I was going, and I knew what I was good at, and the plan was just going to roll on out. I can't think of a more perfect illustration of a fixed mindset.

I then had to learn to adapt to the change that had been forced upon me – and I *did* adapt. I learned how to carve out a new identity as a wheelchair athlete and I refused to let my new circumstances restrict or define who I was. Over the next 25 years I worked hard at developing an open approach to new possibilities, and this growth mindset helped me to represent my country in five different sporting disciplines.

Then, in 2013, I hobbled into Ken Ware's gym on my crutches, seeking help for the chronic pain I was experiencing from an old shoulder injury. For the past two decades he'd been putting into practice a neurophysics theory that he'd developed from his experience as a runner and body builder. In that first session, he asked me what I wanted. Of course I responded that I wanted to walk again, as I'd never completely let go of that dream. It's too complicated to explain in detail here, but Ken believed that, because I was an incomplete paraplegic, I'd always had the potential to walk. According to Ken, my belief that I was a wheelchair athlete had closed my mind to exploring the possibility. His words gave me the courage to open my mind to a different future, and I managed to take my first three unaided steps in 25 years.

On 26 October 2014, I once again competed in the Nepean Triathlon, the race for which I'd been training when I had my accident – and one of my first events as a wheelchair athlete. This time I completed the race with carbon-fibre leg braces and walking poles, but *no* chair. When I was within sight of the finish line, I threw aside the poles and crossed that line hand in hand with my wife and son.

Starting with those first three uncertain steps in the gym 18 months earlier, I'd had to put in a huge amount of hard work to realise that dream – not only physically, but also emotionally. For 25 years I'd been in a wheelchair, and suddenly I could walk again, not smoothly and certainly not quickly, but *independently*. My dream had come true, and of course I was ecstatic, but it did mean a major change in the way I perceived and managed my world. You can't just click your fingers and change your mindset overnight – I once again had to re-define who I was.

With the right mindset, you too can respond and adapt to change and build your dream.

If you change the way you look at things, the things you look at change.

Wayne Dyer

MENTOR

The delicate balance of mentoring someone is not creating them in your own image, but giving them the opportunity to create themselves.

Steven Spielberg

For me, mentors are people who see your potential and have the experience and commitment to work with you to help you achieve your goal. They don't tell you what to do, but they can help you open up your thinking and start to consider new ways of tackling your challenge.

Mentors can emerge from any area of your life, and I've certainly been very fortunate in meeting some wonderful people who've fulfilled this role for me. But there's no doubt that my father's support, encouragement and unswerving belief in me has provided the bedrock on which I've built my career. It's been his words that resonate in my head, every time a new challenge emerges: *How far can you go?* If you're lucky enough to have such a person in your world, then hold them very close.

Trying to make significant change in your life on your own is a big ask. Even for the most motivated, there will be days when it all just feels too hard – when your goal seems ever further away, and each step of your carefully worked-out plan is becoming steeper. Many of us can be too proud to ask for help, thinking that it's a sign of weakness, but in fact the opposite is true. It makes perfect sense to work with experienced people who've successfully negotiated the same hurdles that are confronting you.

So, are mentors and coaches one and the same thing? Technically, coaching is all about performance. It focuses on a set of tasks and the development of new skills. It usually has a defined time frame and can be measured by the attainment of specific goals. Mentoring, on the other hand, is about relationships, which can often span many years. It focuses on personal growth and development, rather than on specific tasks.

But in the end, it doesn't really matter which term you use, as long as it makes sense to you. In my world of support, I use both. Coaches help me develop the physical skills and techniques that allow me to take on the sporting challenges that I love, and my mentors help me develop the attitudes and resilience that keep me going when the going gets tough.

The fundamentally important thing is that you need people in your life who've walked the path you want to take and have the experience and skills that you can learn from to navigate your own change.

When I was starting to develop my plan to swim the English Channel, I met the author Ian Heads, who'd written Des Renford's biography, *Nothing Great Is Easy*. Now, Des was the king of the Channel swim, having crossed that expanse of water an amazing 19 times, so I asked Ian if it might be possible to meet him. That meeting happened, and Des was incredibly generous with his time, filling me in on the realities of what this epic swim would actually entail. I doubt I would have managed to knock that challenge over without his experience to guide me.

In the Sydney Olympics in 2000, I qualified to compete in the 1,500-metre wheelchair event. I was thrilled. A gold medal was firmly in my sights when, 350 metres from the finish line, I came into contact with another athlete, causing my wheelchair to flip and spilling me onto the track. My Olympic dream was over.

That was a big pill to swallow, so, seven years later, when the chance came around again, I set out to recapture my Paralympic dream by qualifying in the mixed double sculls in Munich in 2007. As I'd never competed in this event before, I had a huge task ahead of me and I was going to need every bit of help I could get.

From a coaching perspective, there was much to be done. I rapidly had to learn about adaptive rowing, which meant acquiring a new set of technical skills. But I also needed strong mentorship, to help me make the transition from individual sport to a mixed-gender doubles competition. My mental approach and belief in myself would be every bit as important as those quantifiable rowing skills.

The same thing is true for any challenge.

But it's important to choose your mentor wisely, as not everyone has the willingness and openness to share their knowledge with you. All mentors are *not* born equal. Ask yourself the following sorts of questions:

- *Do you feel at ease with this person?*

- *Have they got experience and knowledge that you would like to emulate?*

- *Do you like them?*

- *Do you share a sense of humour?*

- *Do they share your passion and excitement?*

A strong mentor relationship is a special thing, and it's worth taking the time and trouble to build that relationship with care and consideration. Your mentor will be able to open new doors, not only in your thinking, but much more literally, in terms of contacts and opportunities that you may never have been able to access. For a mentor to open these doors, they need to have total trust that you'll handle all resulting situations with sensitivity and respect – and that kind of trust needs time to grow. So, choose wisely, throw away your inhibitions and allow your mentor to help you make some exciting changes in your life.

A good mentor offers directions and driving tips from the back seat. You still have to drive the car.

Michael Johnson

MOTIVATION

Some people dream of success while others wake up and work hard at it.

Napoleon Hill

Motivation can be defined as *the process of stimulating people to action in order to accomplish a goal*. You need a sense of purpose, but true motivation requires *action* as well as thought.

When I finally got home after my accident, I had a very clear sense of purpose. I'd decided that I wasn't going to be defined by my wheelchair. I was going to use the strength and resilience that I'd developed before my accident to achieve my goal: to excel as a wheelchair athlete.

Of course, nothing's that simple, but looking back I can see there were many influences that helped me build this resolve. I'm a sucker for triumph-over-adversity movies, especially if they involve my love of running. I only have to hear that Vangelis soundtrack music start up to be transported back to one of my all-time favourites, *Chariots of Fire*. And who doesn't feel uplifted by *Dead Poets Society*, when those boys stand on their desks in defiance? Seize the day indeed!

We all have our own bank of great stories that inspire us to keep going, whatever the roadblocks in front of us. Sport is where I find much of my inspiration. Derek Redmond completing the 400-metre sprint at the Barcelona Olympics in 1992, after tearing his hamstring during the race, physically supported by his father across the finish line. Or Jim Ward, lining up for the gruelling Hawaiian Ironman race at the age of 78, and successfully completing the course within the specified time limit.

You need a sense of purpose, but true motivation requires action as well as thought

Then of course there are all those famous entrepreneurs who have suffered more than a few setbacks on their path to success. Sir James Dyson spent 15 years' worth of savings on 5,126 failed prototypes, before number 5,127 became America's biggest-selling bagless vacuum cleaner. Guy Laliberté was a street performer, walking on stilts and breathing fire, but went on to develop the worldwide phenomenon of Cirque Du Soleil. Elon Musk was fired as CEO of PayPal, the company he'd created, before he went on to send astronauts into space.

The list of people who've demonstrated the power of motivation could fill this entire book, and more, but when you read about their success, the same words are used over and over again: *tenacity*, *persistence*, *courage*, *perseverance*. When things went wrong, they simply refused to give up.

You'll have your own list of inspirational people whom you admire, men and women who've also refused to give in to whatever struggle they faced. There are also the people who've continued to love, support and encourage you, even when you feel you've done something unforgivable. The boss who gives you that priceless second chance. The teacher who maintains their belief in you, even when you've lost faith in yourself.

Whether it's a movie, a book, a piece of music or a simple phrase said at exactly the right moment, we all have a reservoir of inspiration we can draw on to help us build that sense of purpose.

I'm a visual person, so I find it helpful to build a picture of what success would look like to me: the finishing tape at the Hawaiian Ironman, the Olympic medal ceremony, walking along the beach holding my wife's hand.

A dream is very important, but it's only helpful if it's linked to action. Dreams won't become reality unless they're realistic, allowing you to maintain a strong sense of purpose. If you want to become President of the United States, it's highly unlikely that any amount of dreaming will get you there.

It's also important to understand that success is not guaranteed. But if you fail to achieve your goal, this is *not* a reason to give up. You may have set the wrong goal, or the timing was off, or circumstances prevented you from giving it your best shot. Whatever the reason, you can learn much from failure or adversity that will help you build even greater success in the future. After all, President Abraham Lincoln failed in business, had a nervous breakdown and lost eight elections; Steve Jobs was fired from his own company; and Nelson Mandela endured 27 years in prison.

So, if your first goal doesn't go according to plan, then *pick yourself up, dust yourself off and start all over again*.

The real test is not whether you avoid this failure, because you won't. It's whether you let it harden or shame you into inaction, or whether you learn from it; whether you choose to persevere.

Barack Obama

MOMENTUM

Unwavering incremental change can create remarkable and monumental results.

Ryan Lilly

The dictionary definition of momentum is *the force that keeps an event developing after it has started.*

This all sounds good, but how do you know if you've managed to build momentum? I think the answer is: when it's harder *not* to do something than it is to do it.

Change takes place by action – and action usually means taking small, progressive steps towards the goal you've set yourself. Positive change is not about a magic bullet, although it would be a lot easier if this were the case. Your old habits have formed over a long period of time, and lasting change means adjusting each of those old habits until your new set of behaviours and responses becomes second nature. Easy!

Actually, I can't promise that. But there are some simple things that will help:

- *Just make a start:* I know that sounds simplistic, but it doesn't matter how good your plan is if you do nothing about turning it into reality. Think about Nike's slogan, 'Just Do It'.

- *Time:* Work out when you're going to start and then take time every day to do something positive towards your goal.

- *Research:* If you find that you're getting stuck, get some help. Read, listen or contact your mentor. Draw on the resources that you've put in place to get you back on track.

There are many, many quotes about momentum and building success, but in discussions about them some common words emerge, which are useful to think about:

- *Failure:* This is mentioned surprisingly often. Success isn't instantaneous and it doesn't always happen first time, however hard you try. The only guarantee is that the failures make the success that much sweeter.

- *Action:* You build success by *doing*, not by talking and overanalysing.

- *Resilience:* We all stumble, but success comes when we pick ourselves up again and keep going. Succumbing to an ice-cream covered in chocolate doesn't mean you should then abandon your healthy eating regime.

- *Love:* Loving yourself and loving what you do are the essential ingredients cited by so many successful people.

- *Positivity:* Focus on what you *can* do, rather than dwelling on what you can't.

- *Choice:* We have free will – we can choose to make a difference to our lives, or we can choose to sit still.

- *Courage:* There's no question that the easiest route is the path of least resistance, but it's not the most satisfying. Having the courage to take the tougher road pays off in the end.

- *Imperfection:* Success is not the same as perfection. If you're only satisfied when you've reached the ideal, you'll never feel you've attained anything.

There's no question that the adage *success breeds success* is true. It's how we build momentum. Every time we reach a goal, it spurs us on to take the next step, and nothing can motivate better than achieving something that was hard won. It might have taken me three attempts to attain my goal of becoming the first wheelchair athlete to complete the Hawaiian Ironman, but when I finally managed it, the triumph I felt couldn't have been sweeter.

Back to the COVID-19 crisis for a minute. It's certainly building momentum at a scary rate, proof positive that bad stuff gathers momentum just as easily as the good things in life. At a time when the world has become such an uncertain place and everything we all took for granted seems to have up-ended itself, it's very easy for that inner voice to come to the fore: *What's the point in doing anything when I don't even know if I'll still have a job once all this is over?*

I'm not trying to make light of what's happening, and I'm certainly not judging your fear and concern about the impact that this pandemic may have on your family and friends. But the effects of an event of this magnitude will be far-reaching, and if you can continue to build your own momentum towards making positive change, you'll be much better positioned to create a meaningful life in the new landscape that will emerge from this horror.

The scale and speed of the change that COVID-19 has brought about has been immense, but even in the midst of this chaos and distress, you still have a choice.

You can *fear* it and try to pretend that it's not happening, or you can *embrace* it and use this time to position yourself to make the most of the future.

In fact, those very times when life seems to smack us in the face – when it feels so much easier to give in than to get back up again – represent the greatest threat to building momentum. The challenge is to stay focused and determined. Your plan may have to change, but there's always another way to achieve your goal. Draw on every resource available to you in order to keep moving forward. Talk to your mentor, learn from what others are doing to cope, and keep that momentum going.

Bravery is not the absence of fear but the forging ahead despite being afraid.

Robert Liparulo

5Km

MOMENTUM

MOTIVATION

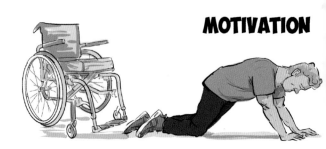

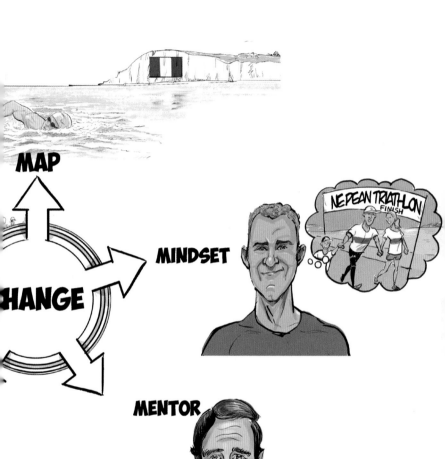

Now, take that first step

My story of change started when I was hit by a truck while training for the Nepean Triathlon, and came full circle when I finished the triathlon 26 years later, once again without my wheelchair. Looking back at how I tackled that event, I can now clearly see my formula for success. I had a MAP and I fully understood the plan: swim 1 kilometre, bike 30 kilometres, walk 10 kilometres. I engaged a positive MINDSET, which allowed me to believe in the impossible. My father was a wonderful MENTOR, who posed the question: 'How far can you go?' My MOTIVATION to keep moving forward was stronger than the pain trying to hold me back, and the MOMENTUM that I built from each step drove me on to the finish line.

Change is unavoidable. Whether we like it or not, we're all going to experience times in our lives when our world is turned on its head and we're faced with choices we may not want to make. There's no escaping the fact that you'll have to make a choice, even if you decide to do everything you can to maintain the status quo. But I hope that my path for handling change can lessen your fear and anxiety, and help guide you to grasp new opportunities and realise your dreams. This methodology has been a winning formula in my life and I know it can be in yours. All you have to do is take that first step.

Thanks

So many people have contributed to shaping the person I am today that it would be a long and involved list to document. But to every person who has been a friend, teacher, coach, mentor or critic: I thank you for your support, words of encouragement and insights. Know that I have taken all my experiences – good, bad and indifferent – and layered them with your wisdom to create a strong and resilient mindset. Over the years I've filtered thoughts through my subconscious in an effort to move away from internal dialogue that doesn't support my goals and dreams, and my hope is that I can now use everything I've learned to support others to do the same.

This year has been particularly challenging for many people. Challenging for me in ways I never considered. In the initial stages of putting this book together, COVID-19 turned the world upside down, and many of us saw our businesses grind to a halt overnight. As I've worked through the chapters and gathered my thoughts and experiences, I've had to use my own process yet again to start thinking about how my business will look in the coming months and years.

I couldn't have articulated my thoughts so succinctly without friend and writer Juliet Rogers. Ju, thanks for your patience, and your patience! Also to my close friend and mentor Ross Cochrane – as always, your insights have been invaluable.

I've always liked the analogy of life being a journey on a bus. There's a driver, and there are passengers, all moving from point to point. I've been a passenger before, and that's allowed me to learn and reflect, to gain insights, and to observe. However, I now know for certain that I'm behind the wheel of the bus. I'm mapping the journey. I'm firmly positioned in the driver's seat.

Who's driving your bus?

John Maclean

About the authors

John Maclean

In 1988, while riding his bike in training for the Nepean Triathlon, John Maclean was hit by an 8-tonne truck. The accident left him a paraplegic. Despite the excruciating physical pain and the challenges of daily life in a wheelchair, John decided he would become bigger and stronger than ever, by proving himself in the toughest sporting events the world had to offer.

In 1995, he made history by becoming the first wheelchair athlete to finish the course at the Hawaiian Ironman Triathlon, continuing to the finish line despite falling outside the able-bodied cut-off time in the bike section. It took two more attempts for him to complete the course within the cut-off times, an achievement that saw him become the first non-American, and the first wheelchair athlete, to be inducted into the Hawaiian Ironman Triathlon Hall of Fame, in 2002.

Success in many more extraordinary sporting challenges followed. In 1998, John became the first wheelchair athlete to swim the English Channel, and in 2005 he completed the gruelling Molokai Challenge, the open-ocean paddling world championships. He represented Australia at the Sydney 2000 Olympics and Paralympic Games, and in 2001 he sailed in the Sydney to Hobart Yacht Race. In 2006, in Hawaii, John took part in the Ultraman World Championships, an invitation-only extreme endurance event.

Early in 2007, John was invited into the sport of rowing. In September 2007, he and his rowing partner claimed a silver medal at the Rowing World Championships, and followed up with gold at the International Regatta in Italy in April 2008. The same year, John won Rowing silver at the Beijing Paralympic Games.

Parallel to his sporting career, John sought to focus his energy and determination on helping others. In 1998, he established The John Maclean Foundation, which is now a national-scale organisation providing support and assistance to Australian wheelchair-users under the age of 18.

In 2013, after working with neurophysics therapist Ken Ware, John took his first steps towards achieving his dream to walk again. In 2014, John competed in the Nepean Triathlon, finishing the course as a conventional athlete.

Juliet Rogers

Juliet Rogers has worked in the publishing industry since her first holiday job in a bookshop, when she was 15 years old. After roles as a book sales rep, marketing manager and sales manager in publishing, she spent nine years as managing director of Random House New Zealand, prior to moving to Australia and running Random House Australasia-wide. From there she spent the next ten years managing Murdoch Books, and then set up her own business, The Wild Colonial Company, working as a publishing consultant and independent publisher. From 2016 to 2020, she was CEO of the Australian Society of Authors.

Juliet has served as president of the New Zealand Booksellers' Association, president of the Australian Publishers' Association, vice-chair of the Australian Copyright Council and chair of the book industry charity, the Indigenous Literacy Foundation.

A John Maclean book for Simon & Schuster Australia

Change: A Constant Challenge
First published in Australia in 2020 by
Simon & Schuster (Australia) Pty Limited
Suite 19A, Level 1, Building C, 450 Miller Street, Cammeray, NSW 2062

10 9 8 7 6 5 4 3 2 1

Sydney New York London Toronto New Delhi
Visit our website at www.simonandschuster.com.au

A catalogue record for this
book is available from the
National Library of Australia

ISBN: 9781760859374

Editor: Diana Hill, Crimson Lane Publishing Services
Designer: transformer.com.au
Illustrator: Mike Bryson, drawnbymike.com
Printed and bound in Australia by McPherson's Printing Group

MIX
Paper from
responsible sources
FSC® C001695

For further information, or to engage
John for personal development
workshops, mentoring or speaking,
please contact
amanda@johnmaclean.com.au